LEARNING MANAGEMENT BEHAVIORAL STRATEGIES

JOHN LOK

Contents

Preface

Introduction

Any organizations must need management strategy. This book explains how and why organizations ought how to implement effective strategies to help them to set up their businesses more easily in the beginning. Students can understand what our businesses need real requirement in order to implement their businesses more easily and successfully in their business birth stage.

Prologue

Table of content

Chapter 3 Learning organizational communication strategies

Q1 Define the term effective communication p.31-40

Q2 Outline how this case could harm employer-employee relationships in this factory in the future.

Q3 Evaluate the different ways in which Panasonic might communicate any future redundancies to staff and the media.

Chapter 4 Learning Leadership Style

Q1 Explain the types of leadership style Pierre and Oscar most closely represent. p.41-50

Q2 Analyze the possible reasons why Le Menu overspends on food.

Q3 Discuss the advantages and disadvantaged to Le Menu of Oscar's style of leadership.

Chapter 5 Learning organizational behavior

Q1 Explain what you understand by the terms: p.51-63

a. motivation

b. responsibility

Q2 Identify two factors that seem to influence job satisfaction and explain them in terms of Maslow's hierarchy of needs.

Q3 Explain in terms of the features of job enrichment why it might be easier for small firms to motivate staff than big businesses.

Q4 Discuss the extent to which it might be possible for large firms to use Herzbeng's motivation to improve the level of work motivation.

Chapter 6 Learning organizational culture

Q1 Explain on possible reason why Sally thought it necessary to change the organizational culture of Regal Supermarkets. p.64-73

Q2 Outline the type of culture that Sally seems to be introducing at Regal Supermarkets.

Q3 Analyze the key steps that Sally should have taken to manage cultural change more effectively.

Q4 To what extent will the change in culture guarantee future success for this business?

Chapter 7 Learning organizational employee and employee relationship

Q1 Explain what is meant by: p.74-85

b. collective bargaining

Q2 Analyze two potential benefits to both workers and employees of a globalise union.

Q3 To what extent would any one multinational company be likely to be affected by the development of one large global trade union?

Chapter 8 learning crisis management strategies

Q1 Define the following terms: p.86-106

a. Crisis management

b. contingency plan

Q2 Outline the key steps BP would have gone through to produce a contingency plan for a crisis such as the Deepwater Horizon.

Q3 Analyze the reasons why the BP share price fell by 50 % following the Deepwater Horizon crisis.

Q4 Discuss the likely benefits and limitations of BP's contingency planning when preparing for any future disasters like Deepwater Horizon.

ONE

LEARNING HUMAN RESOURCE MANAGEMENT

Q1a. Explain human resource management

This is the strategic approach to the effective management of an organization's workers, so that who help the business gain a competitive advantage.

Q1b. Explain recruitment

This is the process of identifying the need for a new employee, defining the job to be filled and the types of staff needed to fill it, attracting suitable candidates for the job and selecting the best one.

Q1c. Explain part time/temporary contract

A contract is a legal document that sets out the terms and conditions governing an employee's job.

For a temporary contract this is valid for a fixed time period, e.g. six months or one year working

period. For a part time job, this is for less than the normal full working week, e.g. 25 hours out of

a possible 40 full time hours per week.

The hourly paid academic contract is a means of permitting flexibility in managing the delivery

of the academic programme. It allows the college to broaden the scope of teaching by including

specialist contributions and more usually, it provides a way of dealing with contingencies, such as

unexpected absence or unplanned but temporary increases in workload.

Q2 Explain benefits to college of workplace planning

Workplace planning means this is the establishment of the staff number and skills of the workplace required by

the business (college) to meet future objectives. Benefits of workplace planning to college school college

management think and plan ahead so that there is time to make major read to strategy if human resources

function can't support it.

Efforts to find school staffs, e.g. lecturers, college office administration positions etc. which need select either

from outside advertisement or inside staff promotion methods is more suitable for someone is difficult to fill college any positions can be started well in advance.

College can advance to prepare which positions are necessary training, which can be identified and found what are necessary training to get skills to work for identified positions.

During the college decides and exact workforce number for every department is needed, it will not reduce any college staffs. For example, science and geography subject departments won't reduce any lecturers next year if college has working planning to predict how many lecturers are needed in these two subject departments. Thus, college can take advantage of natural wastage rather than making redundancies which can be costly and de-motivating and it is bad for college reputation if it often dismiss any staffs suddenly.

What is appropriate for an organization to use depends on how easily it can be implemented and the ease can be implemented and the ease with which it can be tailored to the situation?

Thus, working planning is long term and takes plan in the context of many other internal and external influences, so it is not easy to say whether or not it work.

In conclusion, the benefits of conducting workforce planning are that it helps college to get the right people in the right job of the right time. It allows for a more effective and efficient use of workers and for organizing to prepare for restructuring, reducing or expanding their reducing or expanding their workforces. In additions, the process of workforce planning aids organizations by providing objectives which integrate the various units and allow employees space and time to think about common goals for the future.

Q3 Analyze arguments against offering full time and permanent employment contracts to the new office staff and lecturers

Full time and permanent employment means a contract is a legal document that sets out the terms and conditions governing an employee's job. For a full time and permanent contract, this is valid for permanent period, but it has probationary period to test the employee whether who has skill and knowledge to do the job. For example, three months or one month probationary period and the normal full working week is a possible 30 hours at least.

Arguments against offering full time and permanent employment contracts to the new office staff and lecturers for college employer. It can be costly to make a permanent full time employee redundant if the business (college) doesn't need them any more and it can not allow greater for changing market flexibility conditions, e.g. the enrolling student numbers are suddenly falling in this year.

Select college will need three more administration workers and ten more lecturers. Offering part time and temporary contracts to three office workers which won't need to provide long service pension and full time salaries and insurance etc benefits to them, it can save more expenditure in long term.

However, Select college needs to employ ten more lectures to teach it's science and geography students. Offering full time and permanent employment contracts is more right than offering full time and temporary employment contracts or part time and temporary employment contracts to these ten lecturers because who will not have more motivation to keep good staff to Select college if who know to work temporarily as well as who will feel unfair if who know the old lecturers are working full time employment contract.

Hence, I recommend that Select college can offer part time or temporary variable hour employment contracts to these three new office staff and it also need minimum guaranteed income to give to college new office staff.

Otherwise, it needs to offer full time and permanent employment contracts to these ten lecturers because it's geography and science subject students will increase possibly, so who needs these ten lecturers to teach them for long term.

Q4 Evaluate the best ways for college to select the lecturers.

Recruitment is the process of identifying the need for a new employee, defining the job to be filled and the type of staff needed to fill it, attracting suitable candidates for the job and selecting the best one.

As this college needs to select who is the right applicant when it has new lecturers vacancy. It needs to evaluate which are the best ways to select applicant to fill this lecture positions. I shall recommend that the best ways to this college to select and this recruit the new lecturer applicants.

The best ways to recruit and select the new lecturer applicants for this college include:

The first way is the employing specialist recruitment agency to help it to carry on selecting and recruiting process. It begins to advertise lecturer vacancies, interviewing the applicants who apply these lecturer positions till to selecting applicants who own the teaching skill and knowledge to fill any subject teaching vacancies for these lecturer positions.

The reason is because lecturers need have high educated knowledge and work experience, any specialist recruitment agency is the educational professionals to help this college to find the right applicants to do the lecturer positions. Thus this college can employ lecturers from specialist recruitment agency employment service in the short time and this college doesn't need arrange any subject lecturers who need to spend too much time to carrying on interviewing to select the best lecturers.

Another way is college can employ a recruitment agency who identifies candidates, then the college interviews them and makes the final decision.

Next way is college internet employment method, applicants can enter college website to download their resumes to let this college human resource department to read to select who can be interviewed before the due date.

The final way is the college can do all employment advertisement, interview and select the right applicants to do the right lecturer positions to teach the different subjects by all themselves.

However, I shall recommend that specialist recruitment agency employment is the best way to select lecturers.

College reward framework is based on the principle of equal pay for work of equal value and aims to be

flexible and variable enough to ensure that the college is competitive and able to recruit, support and retain high quality specialist staff to achieve college objectives in terms of learning and teaching, scholarship and research, and knowledge exchange. Thus, specialist recruitment agency employment shall be an efficient and effective recruitment and selection method to develop in negotiation with college senior managers and college recruitment department.

TWO

EXPLAINING HUMAN RESOURCE CULTURE

Q1 a. Explaining delaying

Delaying means that large organizations flatten their hierarchies. Flattening or delaying, as it is also known

typically elimination of layers in a firm's organizational hierarchy and the broadening of manager's spans

of control.

Q1 b. Explaining cultural conflict

Cultural conflict (differences) also exist in the organizational workplace and impact on human resource

management. When one organization's any department exists different countries staffs who work together, large organization will have more cultural conflict occurrence between different countries staffs shall

have different personal ideas, education background and working experience and experience to cause

more cultural difference in large organizational departments. Otherwise, small organizations will

exist less cultural conflict because small number of different countries staffs are needed.

Q2 Why cultural conflict seems to exist in Mitsubishi Motors (MMC) Ltd, Japan car maker?

Mitsubishi Motors Ltd reorganises structural Mitsubishi Motors (MMC), the Japanese car maker,

it is 37% owned by Daimler Chrysler, revealed significant changes to its senior and middle management

structure at a shareholders‘ meeting. The changes reflected between the company's incoming German

managers and established executives who found it difficult adjusting to the new culture.

The restructuring aimed to let some old managers to adapt new management change and other some

old managers were to be offered early retirement.

Victoria Emerson, president announced 60 senior staff advisers who were of an advance age and

made a marginal contribution to the company despite remuneration would be removed.

Then, she was made chief operation officer appointed a 100 team comprising about 25 mainly

non Japanese executives. This team is drawn from different departments, was responsible for overseeing the implementation of the company's restructuring plan.

Some long term service members of Mitsubishi Motors (MMC) Ltd 's middle and upper management resented the presence and power of the company team, all of whom were under 40 years old and who were controlling the strategic direction of it.

The tension between the 100 team (chief operation officer team) and some of MMC 's managers was described as Japanese managers with a job for life attitude. This is not part of German management culture. Thus it will have cultural conflict in possible.

Mitsubishi Motors (Ltd) organizational change emphasizes changes in patterns of behaviour, values, meanings. Thus organizational culture will also change to Mitsubishi culture is often defined as that which is shared by and/or unique to a given organization or group, the social holds together a potentially diverse group organizational members.

Various levels and divisions of Mitsubishi Motors Ltd with have different culture conflict of its organizational hierarchy share a similar viewpoint.

For example, Mitsubishi Motors ltd top executive's commitment is to the value of confronting conflicts and then cited evidence from fiercely argumentative group decision making meetings to demonstrate that Mitsubishi Motors Ltd leaders' values were shared and enacted by power level employees.

Thus, Mitsubishi Motors Ltd cultural change is needed some different countries' staffs will change their culture to adopt any different countries' staffs culture to work together in Mitsubishi staffs culture to work together in Mitsubishi Motors Ltd organizations' strategic, business and operative hierarchy levels.

In summary, culture conflict occurs in Mitsubishi Motors Ltd organization because the different countries managers, staffs occupational, educational, working experience background are very different before who choose to work in this company.

Q3 Analyze possible benefits to MMC of reducing the chain of command through delaying.

Benefits of flattening flow primarily from pushing decisions downward to enhance customer and market responsiveness and to improve accountability and morale. Has flattening delivered on its promise to push decisions downward?

Whether Mitsubishi Motors Ltd have delayer and flattened organizational structure can exhibit were control and decision making at the top. The conventional view of flattening, I find that Mitsubishi Motors Ltd CEO eliminated layers in the management ranks, broadened their spans of control and changed pay structures in ways.

CEO and other members of senior management who make resource allocation decisions that ultimately determine Mitsubishi Motors Ltd strategy and performance . Flattening transferred some decision

managers
to functional managers at the top and flattening is associated with increased CEO involvement with direct reports and the second level of top management .

Corporate structure is as a form of internal governance. Shape how decisions are made and how information is communicated and processed. Another essential element of corporate structure is the compensation scheme that
align managerial incentives and guide decision making.

Mitsubishi Motors Ltd hierarchies have changed dramatically. CEO have flattened the hierarchical structure of
senior management: they delayer and eliminated management levels and broadened their span of control. Many
CEO eliminated the chief operating officer position and increased the number of division managers reporting directly to the CEO. The same CEO also broadened span of control significantly and increase the number of functional managers (e.g. CFO etc) reporting directly to them.

Q4 Discuss possible consequences for efficiency of business of new management structure in Mitsubishi Motors (MML), Japan car maker.

Firms dramatically changes the structure of management compensation by increasing emphasis on performance pay (bonuses, stock options) which is relative to base salaries.

Mitsubishi Motors Ltd is from a multidivisional Japan car maker change to a flattened organization structure firm, increased span structure of control. Multidivisional structure is too much layers and more positions to influence organizational communication.

Mitsubishi motors Ltd has systematically eliminated layers in the hierarchical structure of senior management. Part of this delayer can be attributed to the elimination of key senior management positions.

Thus, possible consequences for efficiency of business of new management structure in Mitsubishi Motors (MML), Japan car maker which include benefits to CEO who has more direct connections deeper in organizations and is potentially more involved in decision making across more organizational units. Thus, division managers' decision making is subject to more direct oversight by CEO assigned who exercises more control and pushes decisions up a form of centralization.

Another benefit, it can create organizational knowledge to solve crises which faces easily. For example, one to uncertainty of the future, Japanese Mitsubishi Motors Ltd had to turn to resources outside the organization for new knowledge and insight and the socio-cultural differences between Japan and the western world resulted in their contrasting approaches to knowledge creation.

Tacit knowledge can't be communicated through manuals or theories. Instead , it is knowledge from Mitsubishi

Motors maker Ltd' s employees knowledge who gained through experience and knowledge linked to their

attitudes and beliefs. individual's ideas are highly value in Japanese Mitsubishi Motor maker Ltd and

suggestions and improvements are judged based on Mitsubishi Motor Ltd staffs' merits and is not by

the seniority or starting of the individuals in Mitsubishi Motor Ltd.

THREE

LEARNING ORGANIZATIONAL COMMUNICATION STRATEGIES

Q1 Define the term effective communication

Effective communication is the exchange of information between people or groups with by written, oral, nonverbal organizational feedback.

Thus, effectiveness communication can help organizations to facility decision making and it can provides information by transmitting the data to identify and evaluate alternative choices, it can provide a release for emotional expression of feelings and is for fulfilment of employees, their work group exchange information with feedback need, it can motivate employees to know what is be done, how well who are doing and what can be done to improve performance.

Q2 Outline how this case could harm employer-employee relationships in this factory in the future.

Panasonic unified communication provides cost effective solutions for small, medium and large business organizations. The solutions combine advanced business telephone products with business clients' user productivity tools, networked directly to standard business application in office.

However, it's organization communicates bad news which can harm employer -employee relationships in this factory in the future. The cause was the voice at the end of company telephone on 16 Oct. which indicated there would be no redundancies among the 2400 strong work force at the Panasonic factory in Cardiff. But two days later, there would be job cuts, limited to several hundred. On 22 Oct , 1300 people were to be made redundant again. It's handling of the affair was bad management practice.

A manager of human resources is not the appropriate man to announce the bad news to let it's factory workers to know the bad news. Hence, who had not already found another job at the time. It is not fair to them.

Thus, this case could harm employer-employee relationships in this factory in the future as below:

It's employee shall lack of trust or management by their employer, it shall cause source of future conflict again, Panasonic management staffs shall lack of respect to their employees for management again, future belief of employee redundancy of rumours could create problems, worker insecurity could result in loss of motivation, trends in low productivity and staff leaving shall increase.

All these factors could harm employer-employee relationships in this factory in the future and in reality a combination of these factors could also harm future relationships between different employees are likely to react in different ways. In fact, the factors could interact and have a cause to effect result in all aspects of Panasonic company efficient and effective operation in the future.

Q3 Evaluate the different ways in which Panasonic might communicate any future redundancies to staff and the media. Refer to all aspects of effective communication, the appropriate sender and receiver, the clarity of the message, the medium to be used and the opportunity for feedback.

Redundancies mean this is job loss due to employee's job no longer being required. This may be because the business re-organizes or because it can no longer afford to employ the employee. Redundancy may be compulsory or voluntary. For legal reasons redundancy needs to be formally stated in a letter, whichever primary method of communication is used. However, I shall evaluate the different ways in which Panasonic might communicate any future redundancies to staff and the media as below:

Suggestion one, group meetings:

Group meeting sender may be a senior UK executive and receivers is groups of workers, e.g. a maximum of 30 worker numbers, the medium is speech and question and answer session, the opportunity for feedback is possible but may be limited.

Meeting advantages include direct questions may be asked and followed up with more questions until full understanding and satisfaction are achieved, the message may be reinforced with caring body language, persuading verbal language speaking used may soften the message and/or be easier to understand. However, meeting disadvantages also include questions may be limited to a few and workers shall lack brave enough to ask questions in front of an audience, time limitation may mean that not all questions are asked, questions thought of after the meeting may not be asked, some workers will have their meeting before others, this can result in incorrect transmission of information and/or the feeling the some workers are considered more important than others.

Suggestion two, One -one-one meetings:

One-on-one meeting sender may be senior department or human resource managers, many managers would be needed to do this for mass redundancies and so the task would need to be split and receiver is each individual worker, the medium is speech and opportunity for feedback is possible but may be limited.

One-on-one meeting advantages include direct questions may be asked and followed up with more questions

until full understanding and satisfaction are achieved, every employee can ask the questions which individually

concern them, the personal importance of each employee is recognised, the message may be reinforced with

caring body language, persuading language used may soften the message and/or be easier to understand.

One-on-one meeting disadvantages include the high stress, face to face situation may be for much for some

workers, questions thought of after the meeting may not be asked, some managers may conduct the meeting

better than others , special training may be needed in advance and this may cause rumours to spread, some

employees have had meeting, so rumours and stress will spread quickly, sequencing of meetings may be

different, come employees will have whose meeting before others, which may give the impression that

some employees are considered some important than others.

Suggestion three, letter:

Letter sender may be a senior UK executive who is helped by human resource specialists and lawyers,

receiver is individual worker, medium is writing, opportunity for feedback is questions could be asked

by letter or by requesting a meeting with direct manager or human resource manager. This would

need to be stated clearly in the letter.

Letter advantages include for legal reasons, redundancy needs to be formally stated in a letter, whichever primary method communication is used, the wording can be made clear and easy to

understand, it is a permanent legal record of redundancy, it can be re-read and thought about

carefully over a period of time before questions, questions may be individually asked and

answered.

Letter disadvantages include it may seem impersonal to employees who may resent it, especially after

long service, letter to a lot of employees may arrive through the postal system on different days, for example,

email isn't usually well received and not all employees may have email, email is sometimes not a

legally enforceable or valid means of communication, the written interchange of questions are answers

can be very long, the language used may be formal and this may make it seems even more impersonal

and uncaring, so some employees may not understand formal language.

FOUR

LEARNING LEADERSHIP STYLE

Q1 Explain the types of leadership style Pierre and Oscar most closely represent.

The type of leadership style of Oscar partner who represents autocratic style at Le Menu catering business.

Autocratic leadership style features include leader takes all decisions, gives little information to staff,

supervises workers closely, only one way communication and workers only given limited information about

the business.

Oscar is a tough, direct manager, who tells workers exactly what he wants and then expects them always

to meet his high standards. If not, he is quick to let them know; he has a reputation for dismissing temporary workers part way through an event. Oscar takes the lead during events.

Pierre is much calmer, preferring to consult with his staff. Pierre is more involved with strategy.

Pierre works with Le Menu's chefs on the type of food to prepare for any event.

The type of leadership style of Pierre partner who represents democratic style at Le menu catering business.

Democratic leadership style features include participation encouraged, two way communication used,

which allows feedback from staff and workers given information about the business to allow full staff

involvement.

Q2 Analyze the possible reasons why Le Menu overspends on food.

The possible reasons why Le Menu overspend on food include the chefs suggest the menu who are not the ones

who control quotes or are responsible for managing the budget, if it employs one costing controller to control

every new menu quotes budget to limit it's overspend, it won't overspend on food in possible;

perhaps most of its food suppliers are expensive to provide food menu for it usually ; quotes may be done by

Oscar partner, whereas it is Pierre partner who works on the menu to do catering operation and management

job in this restaurant. If their communication is poor, the quote and menu may not match; overspends on

food will occur in accident of wrong factors from staffs and these two partners co-operation inefficiently;

quotas are for five course meals with canapes foods and drinks, this may not be fully reflected in the price because these foods and drinks exclude the other different kind of foods purchase and so who may spend

more than the quoted cost. Owing it decide to buy the other different kind of foods which have not compared

the quotes for the food suppliers before.

Q3 Discuss the advantages and disadvantaged to Le Menu of Oscar's style of leadership.

The advantages to Le Menu of Oscar's style of leadership include as below:

(a) Events are probably high pressure . In these circumstances, one person may need to take urgent decisions for

instant action, as Oscar partner manage this restaurant business by himself who don't need to discuss with

Pierre partner to spend much time to make decision to deal any matters. For example,

Oscar is a direct manager, who tells workers exactly what he wants and then expects them always

to meet his high standards in restaurant.

(b) Temporary staff (new or old staff) are not all experienced in working together and it may need a lot of

firm direction. He has a reputation for dismissing temporary workers part way through an event. Oscar takes the

lead during events. Thus, Oscar partner can help his restaurant to reduce salary to pay to the low cooking skill

of temporary chefs and low service standard of waiters etc staff when he feel their working performance can't

achieve his expectation and he shall dismiss them immediately. For long term, salary expenditure must be

reduced from his management skill.

(c) There will be no question about who is in charge or what to do. Oscar is this restaurant only manager to let all staff to know who supervise their job and they need to listen their command how to do every job to achieve whose expectation clearly. So, one to one communication is more easily between Oscar and his staffs. During another partner Pierre has no authority to control and manage restaurant. Hence, Oscar partner won't conflict with another partner Pierre often because who doesn't enquire whose opinion how to manage restaurant staffs and operations daily.

(d) Partner Oscar can lead whose waiters service and cooker staffs to co-operate efficiently because who is a direct manager, who tells workers exactly what he wants and then expects them always to meet his high performance standard. Otherwise, he will dismiss them. Thus he must keep the high performance standard of staffs to continue work in his restaurant to raise the reputation of Le Menu restaurant to every clients.

However, Oscar leadership style also has these disadvantages as below:

(a) Oscar's reputation may stop good workers wanting to work for him because who is a direct manager, who need to tell workers exactly what he wants and then expects them always to meet his high standards. If not, he is quick to let them know; he has a reputation for dismissing temporary workers part way through an event.

So the quality of service may fall, because who will dismiss his temporary or contract staffs easily when he feels who are not the right staff to do the job.

(b) He may de-motivate workers, leading to lack of enthusiasm or lower productivity and the catering
business won't be able to operate if he can't find staffs willing to work for him.

(c) Valuable ideas that come from workers may be ignored from Oscar boss. Thus, this catering restaurant will
be difficult to develop to expand its catering service in the future.

(d) Communication channels may be blocked by unwillingness to talk to Oscar boss if his staffs are unwilling
to reflect whose ideas to Oscar what who feel need to help when who deal these daily job to feel difficult, it will
influence their team co-operation efficiently, e.g. if waiters or chefs teams co-operation can't be efficient,
it will cause it's clients need to wait more time to eat and who will feel unhappy to complaint them, even
client numbers will decrease during to this reason in the future.

FIVE

LEARNING ORGANIZATIONAL BEHAVIOR

Q1 Explain what you understand by the terms:

a. motivation

Motivation means the intrinsic and extrinsic factors that stimulate people to take actions that lead to achieving a goal. Intrinsic motivation comes from satisfaction derived from working on and completing a task. Otherwise, extrinsic motivation comes from external rewards with working on a task, e. g. payment and other benefits.

b. responsibility

This is the accountability for successful completion of a task /project or achievement of a goal / objective.

It is accompanied by the authority (power) to make decisions , but either carries the bad result of things go wrong or carries the good result of things go right.

Q2 Identify two factors that seem to influence job satisfaction and explain them in terms of Maslow's hierarchy of needs.

Maslow's Hierarchy of needs which assumes that what motivates people is unmet needs. According to Maslow, the needs that motivate people fall into five basic categories: Physiological needs are the most basic need, physiological needs are the ones required for survival, then is security needs involve keeping oneself free from harm, next is social needs are the desire for love, friendship and companionship, esteem needs are the need for self esteem and the respect of others, the final level is the self actualization needs(the highest level need), it describes the desire to live up to one's full potential. People may be seeking to meet than one category of needs at a time.

These factors that seem to influence job satisfaction: For example, sense of achievement of job satisfaction and opportunity to develop new skills are belonged to the self actualisation needs level; recognition of work well done of job satisfaction, e.g. status, responsibility, reward is the esteem needs level; working in teams/groups with good communication and making workers feel involved of job satisfaction is the social needs level; contract of employment with job stability of job satisfaction is the safety needs level; income is from employment of job satisfaction is the physical needs and esteem need level.

Q3 Explain in terms of the features of job enrichment why it might be easier for small firms to motivate staff than big businesses.

Job enrichment aims to use the full capabilities of workers by giving them the opportunity to do move challenging and fulfilling work. It may be easier for small firms to motivate because:

Job enrichment which might be easier for small firms to motivate staff than big businesses, the reasons include wider responsibilities may be given these are fewer employees to perform tasks.

Large organizations employ many staff, it is more difficult to give them the opportunity to do move challenging and fulfilling work for any staff motivation ; small organizations of each employee may have to fulfil several functions, but large organizations of each employee may more difficult to have to fulfil several functions ; small organizations of full capabilities of each employee may be more personally and individually recognized and used to compare to large organizations of full capabilities of each employee.

Q4 Discuss the extent to which it might be possible for large firms to use Herzbeng's motivation to improve the level of work motivation.

Herzbeng's motivations mean these are factors that results in job satisfaction. They include five match factors as achievement, recognition for achievement, the work itself, responsibility and advancement factors.

It might be possible for large firms to use Herzheng's motivation to improve the level of work motivation reasons are as employee's achievement is possible as below:

The chance of long term service is as the job uses all of the employee's capabilities fully in large organization is more than small organization; employees' achievement may be recognised by both financial and non financial reward from large firms whose chance is more than small firms. Because large organization can give more chance of financial motivation may include salary or wage increases and bonuses and chance of non financial motivation may include job enrichment and job enlargement and team working and empowerment and interest in the work itself can be a significant motivation, e.g. large firms may offer more scope in technical, scientific or specialist work to whose staff of chance is more than small firms.

Large organizations can have more responsibility to improve the level of work motivation. Responsibility can be a motivator even it doesn't lead to advancement, e.g. caring, medical, pharmaceutical, law, accounting etc professional jobs, the large organizational professional staffs need more safety and security feeling are more than the small organizational professional staffs.

There may be more opportunity for advancement in larger firms through growth (organic or external) and staff turnover and the fact that large firms usually have many levels of hierarchy through which on employee can move. Thus, Herzbeng's motivation improves the level of work motivation can use in large organizations in possible.

However, it also might not be possible for large firms to use Herzbeng's motivation to improve the level of work motivation as below:

The reasons include that achievement may be limited within the job description, bigger firms have less flexibility, recognition for achievement may be limited as in big firms, the recognition process may be highly bureaucratic and slow. The work itself may be below the aptitude of the workers, e.g. graduates.

Responsibility may be limited to the job description and advancement may be slow to come and there may be a lot of competition for higher position.

SIX

LEARNING ORGANIZATIONAL CULTURE

Q1 Explain on possible reason why Sally thought it necessary to change the organizational culture of Regal Supermarkets.

Organizational culture is the values, attitudes and beliefs of people working in an organization that control

the way they interact with one another and with external stakeholder groups.

Sally is had experience in the USA as Walmart's chief food buyer who needs to manager this UK largest

owned chain of supermarket. In fact, she can't accept this UK Regal supermarket organizational culture

so, she uses her USA organizational culture to manage this supermarket.

The possible reason why Sally thought it necessary to change the organizational culture of

Regal Supermarkets include that she hoped Regal supermarket can become a highly competitive national

marketplace where consumers want low prices and fresh goods to attempt to make more profit, to rise

shareholder value after it is sold into a public limited company, to change it's low prices and fresh goods

image, to discourage promotion based on long service and loyalty rather than on ability and results.

Q2 Outline the type of culture that Sally seems to be introducing at Regal Supermarkets.

Autocratic leadership style features include leader takes all decisions, gives little information to staff,

supervises workers closely, only one way communication and workers only given limited information about

the business.

Sally seems to be autocratic leadership style to manage Regal Supermarkets. It includes the following feature:

Power is concentrated among a few people and decisions can be made quickly because there are few people

involved in making them because who dismisses 50% of the directors and key managers who

had been replaced and staff salary pension scheme was replaced for new recruits with flexible pay and

conditions contracts. Staff turnover increased sharply. Thus, managers are judged by result.

Sally tries to adapt the organizational culture of Regal

Supermarket business to allow to be successfully in a highly competitive national marketplace where consumers want low prices and fresh foods.

Thus, hierarchical structures are usually typical of power cultures and motivational methods are likely to focus on financial incentives and bonuses for exceptional performance which can encourage risky and inappropriate decision. These behaviours are an autocratic style leader personal feature.

Q3 Analyze the key steps that Sally should have taken to manage cultural change more effectively.

Sally had experience in the USA as Walmart's chief food buyer. Currently, she needed to manage UK Regal Supermarket which is UK one chain of supermarket stores public limited company. Sally must need to change USA business culture to accept UK business culture to manage this supermarket. I shall recommend that She should to take these steps to manage cultural change if who wanted to manage this supermarket more effectively.

Before this UK supermarket organizational culture was like to a big family because Regal supermarkets has established a culture among its staff that had contributed to its success and growth, loyalty to family managers was very high, promotion was based on long service and loyalty, customer service was a priority, it never intended to be the cheapest shop.

But Sally dismissed many directors and key managers, suppliers' terms were shorten, staff salary and pension scheme was replaced for new recruits with flexible pay and conditions contracts. Staffs turnover increased sharply. Sally's new organizational management changing will influence the old UK staffs can't accept happily.

Thus, the first step, I recommend Sally needed to enlarge on existing positive aspects of the supermarket business to let these old UK staffs to know why who decided to do these changing and whether what the benefits would give to these old and new staffs in the future. It aimed to make who to get confidence to work continually and who won't choose to work in another supermarkets.

The second step, Sally needed to obtain commitment of people at the top level to assist who to manage any departments in this supermarket business. Otherwise, Sally needed to replace them if they did not give full support.

The third step, Sally needed to establish new objectives and mission statement and she needed to communicate to all staffs and encouraged bottom up communication to let them to know what the future direction is and how Sally hoped her staffs needed to follow organizational policy to do daily jobs efficiently.

The fourth step, Sally needed to train old and new staffs in new methods to adapt new organizational cultural changing.

The final step, Sally needed to change staffs reward system to reward based on new value.

Q4 To what extent will the change in culture guarantee future success for this business?

Sally changes this business old culture, this supermarket will get these benefits probably as that

higher profitability makes success more likely because Sally plans try to achieve this supermarket

to be successful in a highly competitive national marketplace where consumers want low

prices and fresh goods from another new management cultural methods, emphasis on performance

is more likely to have the business running efficiently because Sally can decide to dismiss any staffs

easily if who feels their performance are not excellent , so staffs will ensure to work carefully,

decisions can be made very quickly when needed because Sally can dismiss directors and key managers

easily who are the top level staffs, so Sally don't need to discuss anyone when who plans to do any matter,

low skilled personal may benefit from autocratic management because whose each salary is also low, Sally

won't choose to dismiss them easily. Otherwise, the high skilled personal , such as managers and directors

who will be dismissed easily because whose each salary is high, so Sally dismisses them to avoid to reduce

more salary expenditure for long term benefit to supermarket.

However, sally's new organizational management culture can not ensure this supermarket will future success and it is never guaranteed, so Sally ought to bring a USA expert into this UK supermarket who may be

resented because these UK old staffs have been moved from a niche market concentrating on service and family

organizational culture to adapt Sally USA organizational management culture in the future.

SEVEN

LEARNING ORGANIZATIONAL EMPLOYEE AND EMPLOYEE RELATIONSHIP

Q1 Explain what is meant by:

a. single union deal (or agreement)

This is an arrangement to an employer recognises only one union for purposes of collective bargaining.

Negotiations may therefore be simplified, as there won't be a diverse range of employee opinions in the negotiation.

b. collective bargaining

This is the negotiation between employee's representatives (trade unions) and employers and their representative on issues of common interest such as salary/wage payment and conditions of work. As the employees are represented as a joint force there is strengths in numbers and individual workers are less likely to be victimised for standing up for their rights.

Q2 Analyze two potential benefits to both workers and employees of a globalise union.

Swedish journalise Thomas Larsson , in his book "The Race To The Top: The real story of Globalization (2001), stated that globalization is the process of world distance getting shorter, things moving closer. It pertains to the increasing ease with which somebody on one side of the world can interact, to mutual benefit, with somebody on the other side of the world.

The potential benefits to both workers and employees of a globalise union include that:

(a) A globalise union has more powerful collective bargaining power and it gives globalization of worker rights because trade union leaders are worried by the growth of globalisation that has weakened their power and reduce their membership. Because employers can now easily transfer production to low cost countries, the unions' power to bargain and negotiate higher pay deals has been much weakened.

However, a globalise trade union would be able to negotiate with multinationals on behalf of members throughout the world and this might prevent worker exploitation in very low wage economies.

It allows negotiation with multinationals to present transfer of production to low cost
countries and exploitation of worker and it stops companies making changes to pay/
rights in one country without consulting workers in other countries.

Thus a globalise union can threaten to global companies (employers) to treat to pay
the unreasonable salaries/wages to whose staffs and workers unfairly.

(b) A globalise trade union challenges the global forces of capital to raise more job opportunities
to different countries workers and employees to get jobs to do more easily because a globalise
trade union encourage any local companies to expand to overseas to do multinational businesses.
Thus, one country workers and employees can have more job opportunities to move to another
country to work if the local company expanded to overseas to do multinational company business
and globalise trade union is the middleman role to solve conflicts between any multinational employers and
employees and workers when the employees and workers need it to help any time.

Reference

Thomas Larsson, The Race to the Top: The real story of globalization(US: Cato Institute,
2001), p.9

Q3 To what extent would any one multinational company be likely to be affected by the development of one large global trade union?

The reasons would be significant for any one multinational company be likely to be affected by the development of one large global trade union include that :

(a) One large global trade union could standardise of payment and work conditions, it could lead any one multinational company to pay higher costs and less competitiveness, therefore a multinational company could not take so much competitive advantage of cheap labour, which could seriously affect profit.

Any one multinational company could not pay the most minimum labour salaries/wages to its employees in any countries easily, if one large global trade union developed to standardise of payment and work conditions to protect any countries employees to have the reasonable salaries/wages standard level and improved safe work environment in factories or offices or shops or warehouses working locations etc.

In consequence, any one multinational company would spend more expenditure to labour salaries/wages and any one multinational company also needed to rise expenditure to improve whose working environment to be safety to every employee. Thus, any one multinational company's profit would be reduced largely.

(b) Negotiations may take longer and include a lot more international involvement between any one multinational company and it's employees and workers.

(c) Every country's any one multinational company 's employer and employees issues could also change into a worldwide problem more easily.

(d) One set of negotiations may be a lot simpler than different negotiations in lots of different countries from a globalise trade union.

(e) Any one multinational company acquisition or merger would mean a constant stream of change, which could complicate the whole process and interfere with external growth.

(f) Different local costs of living may be very difficult to take into account for any one multinational company.

(g) A globalise trade union reduces the power of a multinational company over its workforce.

The reasons would also be little or no effect on any one multinational company be likely to be affected by the development of one large global trade union include that :

(a) In practical terms, different local laws and living costs may take the process very difficult to put into effect to any one multinational company because different local law and living costs are external factor to influence to any one multinational company indirectly.

(b) In a recession unions may be happy to have jobs for their workers, so may not take advantage of global negotiating power to any one multinational company directly.

(c) Job losses in one country could lead another new job to another country when any one multinational company does local and overseas business both.

In conclusion, I believe that it is significant for any one multinational company be likely to be affected by the development of one large global trade union. The reason is that multinational firms exist because certain economic conditions make in possible for any one multinational company to profitability undertake production of a product or service in a foreign location. Production of a product or service in foreign market is desirable in the presence of protectionist barriers, high transportation costs, unfavourable currency exchange rate shifts or requirement for local adoption to local demand that make exporting from the home country unfeasible or unprofitable.

EIGHT

LEARNING CRISIS MANAGEMENT STRATEGIES

Q1 Define the following terms:

a. Crisis management

A crises goes beyond the normal and causes instability or imposes a change in an organization and it can

threaten its future. The impacts of a crisis are therefore experienced across an organization and the

response requires strategic lead in order to (attempt to) manage and control or direction of events.

Thus, a crisis is a form of sudden impact which happens with little or no warning to any organizations.

The origins of a crisis can either be external , where the organization is seen as a victim of an event

beyond its control (e.g. natural disasters) or internal , where a crisis occurs due to accidents in the

workplace (e.g. technical errors) or due to systemic, preventable errors (e.g. human breakdown accidents, organizational misleads causing injury, or the occurrence of a situation that is

outside the current capacity and experience of the management team, as a result of , for

example, key personnel not being available at a particular point in time).

Crisis management is a term often used to describe the way in which cay organization can handle a crisis.

It is planning relates to get the best position to react to and recover from an emergency, incident reacts

properly and orderly to an incident as it occurs.

Thus, organizations need good crisis management plan to reduce much losses when any crisis occurs.

b. contingency plan

A plan is used by an organization or business unit to respond to a specific systems failure or disruption

of operations.

An organization concentrate on using contingency plan to minimize loss and ensure continuity of the

critical business functions of it in the event of disaster.

It is process of developing advance arrangement and procedures that enable an organization to respond

to an event that could occur by chance or unforeseen circumstances.

Q2 Outline the key steps BP would have gone through to produce a contingency plan

for a crisis such as the Deepwater Horizon.

The British petroleum (BP) company Gulf of Mexico disaster occurred on 20 April , 2010 year, the Deepwater

Horizon drilling rig exploded , killing 11 workers and causing an oil spill that soon became the worst environmental disaster. If it had produced a contingency plan for any crisis, I believe that the Deepwater Horizon disaster would not happen easily.

I shall recommend these key steps for it to produce a contingency plan to reduce any business and life loss from any crisis occurrence in the future as below:

The first step, BP company needs to have strong safety culture. It is the set of values held by employees and it's policies that lead employees to prioritize health, safety and the working environment. Many policies and procedures can affect a Deepwater drilling firm's safety culture and thereby affect employees' actions that could cause a spill. Hence, the top level staffs of chief executive officer and managers to the low level staffs of drilling petrol workers can learn BP safety culture how to work in their working environment safely.

BP can produce a risk analysis to measure all workers whose work environment whether is safe or dangerous in order to permit where their working environment is safe for them to work.

The second step, it needs to produce a crisis communication, it means there are lessons to be learned to all employees about not only what could have been done to prevent the spill of drilling rig accident occurrence, but about how to combat an environment crisis on the public relations. For example, a crisis response strategy is needed to implemented by the BP on Twitter internet media. It aims to achieve effective in using social media to control the public relations. Crisis that resulted from the explosion and oil spill, people will respond and react on social media outlets. Hence, social media is as a platform to express opinion and attitude in the BP oil spill response and BP can collect more useful crisis handling methods to reduce the disaster of accidents occur again.

The final step, BP needs to provide training to workers to rise their skills to use different equipments and using a compensation structure that encourage individuals to make decisions that increase safety. Upper management ought need to implement internal policies that affect safety culture and makes decisions and lower level managers and other employees respond to incentives created by upper management create a link between safe culture and safe outcomes.

Q3 Analyze the reasons why the BP share price fell by 50 % following the Deepwater Horizon crisis.

After the Deepwater Horizon, explosion disaster occurred on April , 2010 year. It had caused the bad news to BP. The bad news included that BP announced to compensate $20 billion amount to victims of the oil spill and

it would not pay every shareholder dividend in 2010 year. Hence, investors would feel it had finance difficult and shareholders felt BP would have loss because who could not receive dividend in 2010 year. It caused it's future shareholders lose confidence to invest to buy its shares, even it's old shareholders would sell their shares immediately. When it's share numbers were decreasing, it would also reduce it's share price fall by 50% seriously.

Q4 Discuss the likely benefits and limitations of BP's contingency planning when preparing for any future disasters like Deepwater Horizon.

The benefits and limitations of BP's contingency planning when prepare for future disaster as below:

The likely benefits of BP's contingency planning can include that:

(a) It will reduce the chance of drilling ring exploding occurrence again.

(b) It will rise the confidence to it's new and old shareholders to continue to invest to it's oil productive business for long term.

(c) It's employees will have confidence to work in its drilling oil rig working environment when who feel their working environment is more safe to work. Otherwise, if it's employees felt who were unsafe to work in its work environment who would leave BP easily , specially, BP's experienced skilful workers would leave BP and found another new employer.

(e) It will build loyalty to public because corporate social responsibility is becoming of great importance and consumers consider more than just its petrol products quality and price when making a purchase.

(f) Understanding exacting how the oil spill was caused and the extent of the damages that resulted, including damages to the natural environment, economy and citizens' health and well being provided evidence as to why people were to dismay by the spill and processing the knowledge that it would have been prevented with some basic safety precaution.

Hence, if it produced a contingency plan, it could give public to have confidence to continue to buy its shares to invest to help it to do business in the future.

However, BP would likely encounter these limitations to implement it's contingency planning as below:

(a) The failure of the America government to assign and in some cases to permit resources to assist

with the containment of the oil spill. Although, it can get these benefits from the contingency planning,

but it still lacks enough funds to repurchase any advanced and safe oil spill productive equipments.

(b) It needs to spend much time and expenditure to provide training to help it's old and new skilful

workers to learn how to control oil spilling equipments easily to reduce human error and

equipments failure in the short time.

(c) The disaster crisis would have been avoided if proper safe precautions were taken.

For example, reducing drilling Deepwater Horizon to be evacuated overnight to cause

fire occurrence chance to the incident. In fact, BP lacked enough skilful workers and

equipments, so it's workers need to work overnight to cause fire.

In conclusion, BP's contingency planning will likely to get these benefits, but it needs to

have more fund to repurchase many advanced oil spilling equipments and paid more

expenditure to provide training to raise it's skilful workers knowledge to control these

new equipments if it wanted to get the benefits from contingency planning in fact.

Printed by Libri Plureos GmbH in Hamburg,
Germany

9 798887 495477